6/12/06
To Laurie
Best Wishes
Al [illegible]

Having surely proven how to succeed in business, Al Marino continues to successfully consult, coach and stimulate self-motivation and self-responsibility in individuals and companies, helping them achieve their challenging futuristic goals. In *Making Anything Possible,* he offers a down-to-earth, common-sense solution to overcoming barriers for us all. This book will most certainly appeal to everyone, no matter who you are or what you do!

—Dr. Oscar C. Christensen, Ed.D.
Professor Emeritus, Counseling and Guidance
University of Arizona

Al Marino has crafted a powerful formula for personal achievement. By emphasizing individual responsibility, Marino unmasks the futility of passing the buck. In doing so, he fashions a clear road map for the one person who is ultimately responsible for your success...you! This book is a must read.

—Dr. Criswell Freeman, psychologist
author of *When Life Throws You a Curveball, Hit It*

The notion of self-reliance and self-responsibility fortunately has once again become valued in our society. Al Marino's book gives us both substance and direction. This book is practical, fun, and the quotes alone are worth the journey.

—Twyman Towery, Ph.D., FACHE
author of *Wisdom of Wolves*

# Making Anything Possible

## Excellence in Self-Accountability, Credit and Blame...

AL MARINO

Leadership Resources Institute
Las Vegas, Nevada

ISBN: 1-886371-30-X
Library of Congress Number: 96-83787

Cover Design: Brad Talbott

Leadership Resources Institute
2251 North Rampart Boulevard
Las Vegas, Nevada 89128
(702) 458-5355

# Dedication

*To Rosalind, my ever-patient wife*
*of thirty-eight years*
*who has endured my dreams and actions.*
*To my 102-year-old father,*
*who on occasion still accompanies me*
*to my clients' offices,*
*stimulating my self-motivation*
*and offering living proof*
*that he is a survivor.*

# ACKNOWLEDGMENTS

*My thanks to Richard Courtney, Currey Copple, Sandy Aud, Brad Talbott, Donna Paz, Criswell Freeman, Eric Kampmann and Harold McAlindon for their help in publishing this book.*

*I also thank the hundreds of companies I have worked and grown with over the last forty years and the thousands of gracious people who have participated in the many and various workshops, seminars and presentations I have delivered.*

*The following special people have had a significant positive impact on my continuing journey through life: Barbara Jean "Bobbie" Alessi; Phil Pace; Richard Hadel; Bill Louchheim; Gordon Bodek; Steve Wallace; Jim, Bob and Jay Delaney; Joe Tom; Dale Smith; Randy Halle; Jerry Epstein; the Al Ghelfi family; and Bob Jenson.*

*A very special thank you to my dear friend and colleague Dr. Carroll Thomas. His inspiration, support and contribution to the writing of this book made it much easier and added quality to its content.*
*A multi-talented, very caring person, he continues to make anything possible and coaches and guides a multitude of others to do the same.*

# Table of Contents

# Foreword

*"These successes encourage:*
*they can because*
*they think they can."*
—Virgil

Religious movement founder John Wesley said, "Catch on fire with enthusiasm, and people will come from miles around just to watch you burn!" That's what happened to Al Marino, and myself. Al caught on fire (actually he naturally sets himself on fire on a regular basis), and I went and watched him burn! Burn he did, and that flame exploded into this book.

Al and I had talked a few short months earlier about an idea he had for a book. I thought it was a great idea and poured on the confidence and encouragement, for I truly believe that Al Marino has a wonderful, and timely, message to present and a unique way of presenting it—as well as an original way of getting it into print! We had talked a lot about all the "victimitis" that seems to be permeating the country—particularly on television talk shows. We agreed that bad things happen to real people—all kinds of bad things to all kinds of good people—but we don't have to make a living at it! As it says in Matthew 5:45: "God makes the sun rise on the evil and on the good, and sends rain on the just and the unjust."

One day I walked out to check my mail at the office of my psychology practice. I found a book cover with Al's picture on it—with no book in between! I called Al and said, "Al, that's a great picture and you look good, but where's the rest of the book?" Al said, "It's already written. It's just in my head!" I said, "Great! Knowing you, I know exactly what it says, but I'm not so sure that everybody else will. Any ideas about how you're gonna get it out of your head and onto paper?" Al joyfully said, "Yep. You're gonna help me. Just come to hear me present it!" I avidly responded, "When and where?"

After about six hours of watching Al burn, at the conclusion of his presentation I said, "Al, you sound like a modern-day Alfred Adler!" He said, "Who's that?" I proceeded to tell him that Adler was the little-recognized Einstein of psychology (in my opinion). Adler believed, as Al does, that human beings by their very nature are *accountable* beings—whether or not they choose to be *responsible* beings. He also believed that human beings are goal-striving creatures—constantly striving toward subjectively perceived positive goals.

Although Al does not formally define his basic tenet as an academic psychologist would, from my perspective his closely matches Adler's basic tenet of *Gemeinschaftsgefühl*, a German word that doesn't translate very well into the English language. It basically means that our highest form of goal-striving is toward being accountable to all of life—not just to ourselves and one another. It involves not only interest in the cosmos and everything in it but "interests in the interests" of everything in it as well. It's really about a genuine interconnectedness, a synergistic communality among all things—animate and inanimate. "No man is an island, entire of itself; every man is a piece of the continent, a part of the main," in John Donne's words. *Gemeinschaftsgefühl*. I love that word. That's Al Marino.

Having come to his own findings independently of Adler, Al didn't know much about the man or his teachings. But as the eager, open-minded student and the fast learner in life that he is, Al generates a genuine kinship to Adler—as you will see from this book. And, fortunately for all of us, the guidance that Al offers as a result of his vast experience in the business of helping people help themselves, others and the world make us all shine much brighter as a result!

I have to tell you, though, that somewhere along the way I think Al got "neglected!" He really seems to have missed out on a few things. For example, I don't think he ever caught the common childhood disease of "Oprahitis." (If you don't know what that phrase means, you will by about Chapter Eleven.)

And I don't think he ever learned to be cynical—or if he did, he got over it or gave it up long before I ever knew him. I don't think he really knows how to be negative or pessimistic. I don't think he's capable of doing anything to hurt any living creature—and I doubt that he could learn to either. It's not that he's not smart enough. Al's one of the most intelligent people I've ever known.

Simply put, Al Marino is one of the finest human beings I have ever had the good fortune of meeting and getting to know and the honor of calling a true friend—a cooperative colleague—a real adventurer on this earth's crust! Find out for yourself by savoring this wonderfully optimistic—and realistic—book, which I have had the good luck of playing a part in creating and for which I have been given the honor of writing this foreword. Enjoy Al's unique wit and wisdom, and treat yourself, as I did, to watch Al burn!

*—Carroll R. Thomas, Ph.D.*
*Las Vegas, Nevada, January 1996*

*"Everybody can accomplish everything provided he has the necessary tools and equipment and the right method can be found."*

—Alfred Adler

# Introduction

Why do some people succeed while others fail? Why is it that ordinary people can accomplish extraordinary things while many extraordinary people manage to accomplish very little?

The answers to these questions began to reveal themselves to me as a child growing up in Los Angeles during World War II. My father was a barber, and he taught me the profession when I was quite young. By the time I was ten years old, I was giving him haircuts and shaves.

Every day after classes, dressed in the blue uniform I wore to the neighborhood parochial school, I would go to my father's shop to sweep up the hair he had trimmed off his customers during business hours.

In the 1940s, a visit to the barber consisted not only of getting a haircut, but also a shave, as well as the prospect of a leisurely game of checkers. Casual conversation usually included the question, "Well, do you think it's going to rain?" Boredom appeared to reign supreme. Fortunately, boredom gave me the opportunity to learn how to entertain myself and stimulate my imagination.

I could have become a successful barber and remained one for the rest of my life. But I discovered at the age of fourteen that I desired something quite different. And I was confident I could have success outside the family business. Why? Because I had learned the principle of self-accountability.

In this book I will explain what it means to hold yourself accountable. It is an opportunity to learn about yourself and the incredible power that accompanies self-accountability. You will find that once you become truly self-accountable, there is no limit to what you can achieve. Your successful journey will be self-fulfilled.

I hope you enjoy learning the one simple principle that can change your life forever, taking charge of your own successes and unlocking the secrets to your full potential through the power of self-accountability as I take you through my own personal journey of putting my dreams into action.

*"One who fears failure*
*limits his activities.*
*Failure is only the opportunity*
*to more intelligently begin again."*

—Henry Ford

# Part I
# A Learning Process

Excellence in self-accountability, like any personal growth opportunity, is a learning process. It begins with what pioneering psychologist Abraham Maslow called being "unconsciously incompetent" in this desired acquired skill. The way we are becomes a barrier, because when we're comfortable with the status quo, we have no interest in change. Therefore, many of us are "unconsciously self-*un*accountable."

* * * * *

One day when I was a young boy working in my father's barber shop, I was staring out the window after finishing my chores . Suddenly, my father broke into my daydreaming by yelling, "Albert!" (He definitely got my attention, as I was not fond of my formal first name and did not enjoy hearing it blurted out for all to hear.)

"Bob Radish, the neighborhood plumber has died," he continued. "He's at Gullick's Mortuary. Go down there and give him his last shave." Mr. Radish had been top-notch in his profession and was well-known and liked by all of us. Still, I was nervous about the assignment.

"But Dad, he's dead."

"Don't worry about the dead people, son. It's the ones walking around who should concern you!"

That was where my career was supposed to begin: I would become a barber. I felt secure and comfortable knowing that being a barber is an honorable profession. I would learn my father's trade so that I would not be a burden to society or to my parents. Indeed, I could even barter the skill for food, as my father had done during the Depression.

However, pondering what was in store, it occurred to me that my future, good or bad, right or wrong, was being decided for me. I was holding myself accountable for another person's dreams, not my own.

Was being a barber what I wanted to do? What were *my* hopes and expectations for *my* life? And how could I achieve them? I realized then that I had to be accountable to and for *me*. Thus, I had made progress by passing through the stage of being "unconsciously self-*un*accountable" to become "consciously self-*un*accountable" and was now struggling to become "consciously self-accountable."

Money was quite scarce for my family, so I decided to get a job. The unemployment office was close to our home, so I went there, in search of opportunity. Because I didn't meet the age requirement of sixteen, I made up a story about my father being dead and my mother being ill just so someone there would try to help me. The man behind the counter indicated that he didn't believe I was sixteen, but he also inquired about my job skills. When I told him I could do anything, was willing to do anything and was anxious to do anything, he shuffled through his 3x5 cards and picked up the telephone. A company owner gave me a one-day opportunity to try out for a job at his trophy business. That was the true beginning of my career and the beginning of my growth to what Maslow would call *un*consciously self-accountable. As a review, the steps to this desired skill are:

1. unconsciously self-*un*accountable
2. consciously self-*un*accountable
3. consciously self-accountable
4. unconsciously self-accountable

*"I feel like I fell*
*into the luck bucket."*

—Pam Tillis

# Chapter One
# Fell in That Bucket Again

I almost called this book *Falling Into a Bucket of Cow @#%& and Coming Out Smelling Like a Rose*. My alternate choice for a title was *Phil: He Did It Again!*

My very special friend Phil has the unique ability to turn everything he touches into gold. As a result, he owns almost the entire city of Montebello, California. But because of his success, he is subjected to criticism by people who declare that he just fell into it—that he didn't earn it by the "sweat of his brow" or by his ingenuity. In the eyes of these detractors, he is viewed as unqualified. They say he just happens to be this lucky person with a beautiful cloud that floats above his head. Every time he picks up a piece of property, even though it's condemned, some other entrepreneur comes along later and wants to buy it from him—for five million dollars!

All my life, I have heard people say that successes

happen more by accident than by plan. Now, these people don't come out and say, "Yeah, you're successful, but you need to know it was an accident. After all, you're dumb and incompetent, and you don't know anything. You're just plain lucky. And by the way, you ought to go to the racetrack."

No, they don't say that. They say things like "Well, you had good fortune" or "God must be watching over you."

Those statements have been two favorite phrases of my in-laws. I think my father-in-law, who is now deceased, still would be convinced that there is no substance to Al Marino. He used to say, "Al is just twenty-six miles of bull, and everyone knows it's going to take him twenty-seven miles to get there!"

Both people have been very important to me. My wife's mother, even now, will tell me, "There, you've done it again. You fell into a bucket of manure and came out smelling like a rose!"

For thirty-eight years, I have listened to such comments. But do they get to me? No, because I know that successful entrepreneurs, on a regular basis, are accused of having the Midas touch or pure unadulterated luck on their side.

* * * * *

*"Two frogs jumped around the rim of a pot filled with milk. Suddenly they both fell into the milk. One of them cried, 'That's the end of me,' and, croaking, made ready to drown. The other did not give up. He kicked and kicked until he felt solid ground under his feet once more. What had happened? The milk had turned into butter."*

—Aesop

* * * * *

For those who are willing to begin the journey to self-accountability, a typical scenario might be:

"I think I'm going to leave retail."

"You're going to leave retail? You've got to be kidding. You're the major force behind the expansion of the Akron Department Stores, a chain that's destined to be gigantic. Why, at twenty-four years of age, with such a career going, are you going to turn your back on that? Don't you realize how fortunate you are to even have a job? Don't you know that people would love to have your position? What are you going to do?"

"I'm going into the manufacturing business."

"What do you know about manufacturing?"

"Nothing.... That's why I'm going into that field! I'm not having fun anymore in retail, and I think I'd like to learn more about the import business. I know I can contribute as much to it as I have to retail."

This scenario is a perfect illustration of what we

can expect when we venture outside society's norms of security. Almost everyone will think we've lost all our common sense.

Years ago, I took a position as a buyer with my own idea of what the description of that job might be. After all, a buyer has to be someone who purchases things from other people, right?

Well, in a manufacturing environment, a buyer must learn about 6061 T-6 aluminum alloy and 302 stainless steel, sheet and plate machines and machine tooling, as well as all kinds of office supplies, Addressograph accessories, fine printed literature, not to mention countless other items.

I had been in the job for a full two weeks when they fired the purchasing agent and put me in charge of the department—another example of falling in the bucket and coming out smelling like a rose. During my six years with the corporation, we established a national representative organization to increase sales. The company, the Bobrick Corporation, is the oldest and largest manufacturer of washroom accessory products. We all use their products.

When I left that position in 1966, I was on the same sort of quest as illustrated in the preceding story. I wanted to learn more and to be challenged.

"They just gave you a thousand dollar bonus!"

"Yes, a thousand dollar bonus is even bigger than a house. I realize it is a lot of money."

"Why would you walk away from the Bobrick family?"

What no one realized was that I wasn't walking away. They were and still are my dear friends. I worked well with Bill Louchheim, who taught me the analytical skills I have which didn't come naturally. He has also taught me that what I often thought was a trivial matter is quite vital. I've learned the purchasing side, the manufacturing side, the supply side and the sale side. Still, there's another marvelous world out there called distribution.

Once again, I was going to do what people have encouraged me not to do. I abandoned my *comfort zone*.

* * * * *

Someone once said, "Success comes in cans." I believe, however, that success comes in all sizes of buckets. We don't fall into them, though. We open them up like a gift under the Christmas tree—when we get outside of our comfort zones. And as Henry Ford so simply said, "Whether you think you can or think you can't, you're right." It's your decision which bucket to take.

More importantly, as you become self-accountable and start to achieve your goals, get comfortable with the knowledge that people won't attribute your successes to you.

*"If you try to explain what*
*the color white is to a blind man*
*and tell him it is like snow,*
*he will understand that white*
*is wet and cold."*

—Willard and Marguerite Beecher

# Chapter Two
# What Is It You Do?

"What do you do?" This polite question is posed, time and again, in social settings as a method of becoming acquainted with another person.

The difficulty comes in formulating the reply. In fact, I'm writing this chapter to answer that query from my 102-year-old father, who still asks me about my current work on a regular basis. By now, you might think he'd have an answer outlined in his mind, but he still delights in hearing me compose the reply. I even commissioned a brochure to explain what I do for a living. Armed with that piece of information, I was certain my father would understand my chosen profession. After studying the contents, his only reply was, "And they pay you for this?"

The question, "What is it you do?" is asked either literally or figuratively on a daily basis. The responses we give contribute to the ongoing image others build on to evaluate our worth and success. This expressed or implied interest—well-intentioned or not—is the greatest favor people do for us. If we are properly and accurately prepared to reply, our well-defined response becomes the basis for what we should be holding ourselves accountable for. In a world of rapid and constant change, we also must continually ask ourselves if we are actually updating or just giving answers that make what we do sound like simply the same old, same old?

Consider the answer you currently give to the question. If you find that you aren't continually changing your response or that it lacks definition, you're not growing. It's important that you understand what it is you "do," for your own self-definition if nothing else. And, you would be wise to continue to modify that definition as you change your life choices. If you're not happy with your answer to the question, you're probably comfortably holding yourself accountable for much less than you can achieve. And you're limiting your continued success if you do not re-evaluate your self-response on a regular basis. Our success becomes a self-fulfilling prophecy of how we think about ourselves and what we say to others in response to this question. Descartes had it right. I not only "think, therefore I am." *I become what I think I am*. Richard Bach eloquently states: "Within each of us lies the power of our consent to health or sickness, to riches or poverty, to freedom or slavery. It is we who control these and not another." Thus enters the importance of self-accountability.

* * * * *

Gene went to school to become an accountant. At the age of twenty-eight, he came to the conclusion that accounting wasn't really enjoyable for him as a career. He made a decision to go into sales and is now the senior vice-president of a national sales organization. The decision surely brought with it the same skepticism and doubt as our previous examples. His success speaks for itself. He became someone who invented the future—a proactive visionary. He exhibited the courage to start over in his career choice.

* * * * *

If you're truly interested in yourself and your continued success, then you had best be asking yourself what it is you do. Prepare to respond positively, comprehensively and accurately. Your answer tells you who you are and governs your sense of accountability. Play with this question frequently. And as Alfred Adler said, "Trust only movement; what a person does is what he means."

*"Be a lamp unto your own feet;*
*do not seek outside yourself."*

—Buddha

# Chapter Three
# Where Is All the Encouragement?

Where do you look for encouragement? And how many times have you allowed yourself to become discouraged by the sources available to you?

* * * * *

Norman says that Sally, his wife of fifty-five years, has never told him that he did anything right. As a very successful entrepreneur, he has found her pessimism to be a pretty accurate gauge for opportunity. "If she says it's a bad idea, I do it," he says. "If she says it sounds good, I reconsider and don't do it."

* * * * *

You won't find the kind of encouragement you need anywhere but inside yourself. Any encouragement that comes from outside sources (e.g., spouse, friends or colleagues) will come with quantifiers and qualifiers: "That's admirable, but...;" "You're so lucky that way. However...."

Ironically, family-owned organizations have to work harder on fostering encouragement than others. Often the parent does not feel the child is ready to step into the business and thinks the company will flounder under his or her leadership. However, when the next generation is given an opportunity and proper guidance, he or she can often take the company to greater heights and success.

You have to be your own biggest fan club. You have to believe in yourself and consider yourself the most important person in the world. Ask yourself, "What are my greatest strengths? And on the other hand, what are my greatest opportunities for getting even better?" Your answers will give you a base, a foundation, as you start addressing the questions and becoming comfortable with knowing what you do.

It's definitely true that the really good stuff comes from within. I encourage you to maintain a "success book." List all your goals and your accomplishments in achieving those goals. Wallow in your successes. They need to be recorded and savored. Refer back to the book often because most of us tend to dwell on our shortcomings instead of the good stuff. The whole idea of identifying specifically what it is we are going to accomplish and then going about doing it is like a snowball rolling down a hill. People grow through their own inspiration as a result of attaining first simpler and then more complex goals. This proactive can-do approach builds self-confidence.

Were you ever on the cheerleading squad while you were in school? Whether you were or not, your opportunity to cheer long and loudly for your favorite person is about to become reality. Since any encouragement you get from well-wishers as you work on the evolution of your answer to "What is it you do?" is likely to be highly quantified, draw on your inner strength as you pursue your goal.

Again, it all comes back to self-accountability. You will provide the unqualified encouragement you need to reach your dreams—you and yourself alone.

*"Argue for your limitations and you can keep them."*

—Richard Bach

# PART II
# I HAVE A PROBLEM?

Over the years, in sharing with many people, I have seen that the common thread among all us is what I have already referred to as unconscious self-*un*accountability. We just don't realize that we might be in a rut, like a car stuck in the mud. And if we work hard enough at it, we can continue to develop all kinds of reasons why it's not our fault that we're standing still. As Adler once said, "When one needs an excuse, most anything will do!"

We often confuse the rut with the horizon.

To help us to identify the horizon, one of the exercises I use with participants in the seminars I conduct is to have them evaluate their strengths and weaknesses. This gives them a basis for building more on their strengths and for turning their weaknesses into strengths. Until one is aware of his or her own personal abilities, it's impossible to concentrate on making any changes, and this perpetuates staying in the rut. Failing to identify weaknesses and develop a plan to overcome them is like asking a contractor to build a house without any blueprints.

* * * * *

Back in 1988 Bob came to a two-and-a-half day Socratic workshop where intense feedback is given. His particular branch operation of a large national distribution company was producing approximately $38 million in gross sales annually. After one day of hearing feedback from his subordinates (people from whom we had solicited anonymous input before the seminar), he had just about had it.

By his own admission, and from recent testimonials he has cited, the big change came in his life on the second day. He realized that even though he was successful, he had gone through his life trying desperately to change everyone but himself. Now he is president of the company's $400 million branch. This success was brought about by his taking a totally different approach to the company's employees, business strategy, marketing, distribution and measurement of productivity—all the things he had previously felt others had to deal with.

The change also impacted his home life and greatly improved his interaction with his wife and daughters, to whom he was not always close. I still work with Bob and his employees, and it is a pleasure because I still see Bob taking charge and continuing to facilitate success and happiness by being self-accountable.

*"A man learns to skate by staggering about and making a fool of himself; indeed, he progresses in all things by making a fool of himself."*

—George Bernard Shaw

# Chapter Four
# Work to Welcome "Wobblies"

It would be simple for me to suggest at this point that everyone attains success and that all people achieve their goals and objectives. However, this statement would not be true. Why? Fear of failure looms like a forbidden monster above our personal growth goals. We become paralyzed when considering mileposts that stretch outside our comfort zones. Our psyches reject the idea of allowing the body to experience what I fondly refer to as the *wobblies*. Wobblies are the weak-knee sensations we get, along with the butterflies in the stomach, when we're about to try something outside our usual mode of operation, our *comfort zone*. We do not want to take risks that frighten us.

After all, just coping with daily life is scary enough, right? Yes, but no wobblies mean no growth. Remember that first time on a bicycle or trying out roller skates or blades? You wobbled at first, but your skill improved with practice and repetition. As fitness instructors quickly remind us, "No pain, no gain."

The fear of failure is the greatest barrier to success. So too is the fear of being successful. Some individuals are skeptical about their best effort being enough and think someone will always expect even more from them. In my seminars the expression of this fear is never explicit, but its presence is sensed by the participants when we do feedback afterward. For example, someone might say, "I never liked the idea of being the chief financial officer. I think I like the idea of being the controller instead. I don't need the extra frustration or headaches." It was William Shakespeare who told us that such fear "makes us rather bear those ills we have, than fly to others we know not of."

Complacency, too, will often overcome any challenge we might consider. I cannot prove it to be a genetic trait, but it seems to endow us all with its presence. We work very hard to maintain a high degree of comfort. When things seem to be going well and we're on a fairly even keel, why would we want to welcome change?

Mao Tse-tung told us, "We must not become complacent over any success. We should check our complacency and constantly criticize our shortcomings, just as we should wash our faces or sweep the floor every day." Complacency, indeed, is often a constant companion and enemy! The wobblies are our only weapon to fight it!

*"The devil made me do it*
*the first time.*
*The second time*
*I done it on my own."*

—Waylon Jennings

# Chapter Five
# Destroyer Phrases

We've all heard the destroyer phrases "You can't" and "Yeah, but...." In fact, we've all used those same words. Worse than that, we've fallen victim to the power of those same expressions, and we have victimized others with their implications.

"You can't do that."
"You will never achieve that position."

At major corporations throughout my career I was told, other people were told, and we told people all the time, "You can't do that."

Have you ever heard of NuCore? If you pick up a *Fortune* magazine, you will see that NuCore Corporation has achieved the number one position on the Fortune 500 list. What made it so outstanding was its perseverance in developing a steel production process whereby the steel could be extracted from a machine but still take up much less space than had before been possible. The discovery was revolutionary and amazed the best engineering minds from Italy, France and Germany.

To borrow from Joel Arthur Barker, "If you think it can't be done, get out of the way of the people who are doing it."

In planning this book, I created the cover before the book was even written. I was asked many times, "Why don't you write the book before you develop the cover? You can't do it that way."

My reply was "Well, why not?" The real challenge is in creating a demand for the message. The book will be of little value no matter how beautiful the cover, how marvelous the words or whether it takes me five or ten years to write it, if no one buys it.

Many intelligent individuals in this world have incredible ideas but are unable or unwilling to communicate their thoughts. They buy into the destroyer phrase that surrounds them. But the fact is "either lead, follow or get out of the way!"

In business the destroyer phrases are ever-present. "What do you mean, get a new computer system? Where are we going to get the money? In this economy? Have you looked at the financial statement?" The attitude permeates all phases of our lives. An easy exercise to become more acutely aware of these phases is to keep a notecard in your pocket and write down every "can't do" comment you hear. How quickly does it fill up?

*"In prosperity, prepare for change;*
*in adversity, hope for one."*

—Evan Esar

# Chapter Six
# Whoa, Here Comes Change

Recently, the president of a major national manufacturing corporation related his own experiences with many employees: "There are a lot of people who are as good as they want to be and you can't make them get better."

I am convinced that more than half the world would be happy if they woke up tomorrow and found we had passed legislation forbidding change! They would delight in something I read about the U.S. Patent Office. Apparently, in the late 1800s it published the information that everything that was going to be invented had already been invented.

I constantly remind my clients that one must experience continual growth. Without growth, the alternative option is quite limiting: you either grow or you die.

By definition, personal growth begins with you

identifying what you are really good at doing and defining what areas of your life need to be improved. And personal growth requires lots of wobblies.

Think of your high school or college reunions. Invariably you run into classmates who stopped growing when they graduated. They still sound like the same person they were then. Some of them echo the sentiments, "I just never got the breaks" or "My ship never came in."

Believe me, I did not grow up in a mansion atop a hill, and my family was anything but wealthy. Our 1929 Chevy wasn't driven because of the fuel shortage created by World War II. We raised our own chickens, and my mom was a four-star chef when it came to making eggplant taste like veal cutlets. Getting certain breaks early in life is irrelevant to future success. You are accountable for your success; no one else is.

* * * * *

My employment with the Bobrick Corporation was a tremendous personal growth opportunity for me. A gentleman named Gordon Bodek plucked me from the manufacturing/supply side and got me involved in sales.

Gordon was probably the first true futurist that I have had the pleasure of working with. He had been a dancer who originally moved to California aspiring to appear in a movie with Ginger Rogers. But because he was so tall, he was discouraged from pursuing a career in dancing and film. As he did some networking to find a new profession, he discovered the Bobrick Corporation.

As I mentioned previously, the Bobrick Corporation is the oldest and largest manufacturer of commercial washroom accessory products. Gordon was given the opportunity to take what was then a soap-dispenser manufacturing company (the original product held either liquid or powdered soap and hung on the wall) and turn it into a maker of top-quality commercial washroom accessories, including paper towel dispensers, toilet partitions, and so on. With hard work, dedication and vision, he developed a national and international company. Gordon was one to emulate and many have. He had no difficulty saying, "I think I did that wrong" or "It was our fault," rather than placing the blame elsewhere. He admired innovation. Eventually, he became president of the company.

* * * * *

People who resist change can also be reluctant to continue learning. They learn as much as they want and then stop seeking more knowledge. Even in their professions, they're not enticed by financial raises or intimidated by potential loss of a job.

We must be clear on our goals and we must remain committed to them. The key is to hold ourselves accountable for both credit and blame as we assess our progress (or lack of it).

At this point you might be wondering, what about everyone else (in the country, in my family, in my life). We get to this in Chapter 15, but I assure you delegation is very much a part of the self-accountability process. Yet we must accept the credit and the blame.

*"One always finds only*
*that which one knows."*

—Charcot

*"We see what we look for.*
*We look for what we know."*

—Goethe

# Chapter Seven
# PERCEPTION *IS* REALITY

If the title of this chapter bothers you, you may find it especially difficult to hold yourself accountable and to take the credit and the blame for your successes or lack thereof. The following four precepts are inevitably true:

1. You are what you look like.
2. You are what you say and do.
3. You are what you don't say and don't do.
4. Anything else, no one else will understand.

If I think that I'm the most handsome devil anyone has ever seen, but I'm the only one who believes that, where is the reality? Forget the old cliche of "seeing is believing." Harold Mosak had it right: "Believing is seeing."

You may believe that you are what you think and feel and that everyone else just doesn't understand you. But what do people see? What do people hear you say and see you do? Your outward self is the 10 percent that shows. No one can see what you think or feel what you feel; they can only make assumptions from the things you say or do or don't say or don't do. To the world, you are what you look like and act like. In order to be perceived differently, you must look and act differently.

To further illustrate the issue that you are what you look like or what you say and do, consider the following:

Picture an iceberg in the middle of the ocean, the ocean representing a fairly flat horizontal surface of water. Further picture the ocean's surface being pierced vertically by the tip of the iceberg, showing triangularly only 10 percent of its overall height. (It may help to sketch what I have described.)

Now, consider that the tip of the iceberg is what you are continually showing. That 10 percent is your noticeable actions (what you do) and what people hear you say. They literally cannot see or hear your inner feelings or what you think (your thought process). They further cannot see your inner values and priorities. In fact, they cannot see your needs. All of these are analogous to our inability to appreciate the size of the rest of the iceberg (below the water line).

The important thing to understand is that people form opinions of feelings, thinking, values/priorities and needs from the aspects of an individual that show, from what an individual does and says. It has been scientifically proven that others' perceptions of us are their reality. When we say, "That's not the way I really am" or "Most people see and think of me that way, but I don't think or feel that way," we are not holding ourselves accountable. Perception is reality, and it will serve you dramatically well if you can get comfortable with that fact.

The major breakthrough in significant personal growth occurs when you're willing to freely accept that the only person you can change is yourself. If that change is not evident or noticeable to others, you haven't changed. (Remember what the iceberg did to the Titanic.)

Becoming expressive and able to communicate ideas is one of the best rewards of change. Communication is about 80 percent of what makes people effective in anything they do. If I can get people to convey meaning and obtain understanding with peers, subordinates and their own families, I have accomplished my goal.

Additionally, if a corporation has communicated clearly its mission statement to all employees and if employees have been involved in that process and understand their own job descriptions and the goals they are to achieve (through regularly scheduled reviews), the company will achieve increased success.

In my seminars, the more analytical personalities are often the toughest ones to convince. If we're discussing how to sell an idea to upper management, they'll say, "If it's a good idea, it will sell itself." I'm here to tell you that's simply not true. Good ideas do not sell themselves. In fact, good ideas often go unspoken and, therefore, unknown. The person who is able to verbalize a concept to a manager is the one who will see his or her idea used.

* * * * *

John had the best idea of all the people in production for cutting costs. However, when he heard that someone else had already come up with an alternative plan, he took his idea home with him and said to his wife, "Guess what they've decided to do now?" Who was responsible for John's idea not being given a chance? Does the word *accountability* come to mind? John is miserable knowing that his idea was better than the one chosen. Management doesn't know anything about it because they were not aware of John's brainstorm. Now John can mope about how he could have really fixed the company. He thinks it's their fault. Of course, it isn't. His idea needed to be expressed in order to be exercised.

*"A man should learn to watch that gleam which flashes across his mind from within, else tomorrow a stranger will say with masterly good sense what we have thought and felt all the time, and we shall be forced to take with shame our opinion from another."*
—Ralph Waldo Emerson, Essay on Self-Reliance

*"Your talent is God's gift to you.*
*How you use it is your gift to God."*

—Author Unknown

*"You are never given a dream*
*without also being given the power*
*to make it come true."*

—Richard Bach

# Chapter Eight
# Is It In God's Hands? Self-Faith

"Destiny. It's destiny."

"It's all preordained."

"Our path has already been established for us by a higher order."

"Trust in Him and He will provide."

"Through my faith, everything will work out."

In my estimation, more than half the world believes that all events are predetermined and that it doesn't matter what you do or say. The inference is that some higher power has total control. The sad part of this is that these people, as they flock to their places of worship, are turning all their success over to God. In effect, they're saying that if it doesn't happen, then it isn't what God wanted. Or if it does happen, and it turns out badly, that's the way God wanted it. This kind of self-satisfying cop-out negates the genuine responsibility people could be taking for their own lives.

People go to church and pray to win the lottery. When they do meet God, they will probably express their disappointment that they didn't win. "Why did you forsake me? I prayed as hard as I could and lit all the candles in hope of winning!"

If two boxers step into the ring and the fighter in one corner is leaving the fight up to God while the one in the other corner is not. Instead, he has developed great self-confidence by using God's gift of athletic ability and training diligently, learning as much as possible about the skill and preparing himself physically and mentally for the challenge. Who is going to win? The winner will be the one who knows how to fight the best using God's gift and his own hard work and who wants to win the most, holding himself accountable.

Dogmatic sayings are invoked by human beings occasionally and they do provide solace. But it's important to take special care that they do not become cop-out phrases. You must have faith first and foremost in yourself. You can't have true and honest faith in God if you don't have faith in yourself. It's essential that we work in conjunction with our faith to achieve our goals.

Each of us is endowed with marvelous gifts, but it's up to us to use them properly. If we don't do anything with them, I believe it's safe to say that God will be more than a little disappointed.

As a friend's mother used to say, "God helps those

who help themselves." You are your most powerful resource and ultimately accountable for what you do. Have faith in yourself.

*"If you had to have a rule*
*for swallowing,*
*you would choke*
*to death."*

—Alfred Adler

# Chapter Nine
# Making It Confusing and Difficult
## or
# Bigger and Better Excuses

Remember the wobblies? (See Chapter Four.) The wobblies are very much with us every time we decide to make our goals primary in our focus. In fact, we're so nervous about that initial step, we inevitably find the biggest barricade we can and plant it firmly in front of ourselves.

* * * * *

Several years ago, Jean went to work for a company that was spending $65,000 on a computer. She quickly learned, however, that some of the basic tenets for any corporation did not even exist at this establishment. The business had no organization chart, no one knew who their supervisors were, there was no distinction between buying and selling, and pricing structures were nonexistent. The whole purpose for buying the computer seemed to be so the company could use it as an excuse for the lack of discipline in all other areas. The perception was that a computer would organize us. The computer was being held accountable, not the company.

Bigger and better excuses (so we don't look stupid) shift accountability onto something or someone else. Always following the rules can quickly become one of our biggest excuses for not stepping out.

* * * * *

A mother was attending the yearly Fourth of July parade along with some of her friends. Her freshman son was marching for the first time with his high school band, proudly playing the tuba. As the band progressed down the street and approached the reviewing stand, the mother could contain her excitement no longer. "Look," she exclaimed, "everyone is marching out of step—except Tom!" Tom had the courage, in his mom's eyes, to step out and be noticed—to stand out in the crowd. Fortunately for us, "Every crow regards her chick as the blackest and the best."

* * * * *

I believe it was Einstein who said the reason more people are not scientists is because they believe everything scientific is so complicated. Look at the basic concept behind the computer. Its logic is based on the binary system of 0 and 1. When one reduces a formula to its simplest elements, it's not as difficult as it first appeared. But we must be willing to try new and different ideas. Flexibility is the key to any new behavioral pattern. Leadership becomes the key, and self-accountability in leadership means the difference between success or failure.

*"When one door of happiness closes,*
*another opens; but often we look*
*so long at the closed door that*
*we do not see which one*
*has been opened for us."*

—Helen Keller

# Chapter Ten
# Paradigms Become "Screenery"

Webster's Dictionary defines *paradigm* as a pattern or a prototype, a model or archetype. It's an idea about how we think things should be. Joel Arthur Barker assisted us by reviving this significant word but is not an unfamiliar concept to any of us. In grade school we were given a prime example of people and paradigms, the story of Christopher Columbus. People thought he was mad to challenge the notion that the world is flat. Earth as a flat object comprised their perception of what could or couldn't be accomplished when traveling on it.

A paradigm shapes the rules and regulations that govern our perception and ultimately become our "filter system" for processing data. However, these rules and regulations do constantly change. There will always be new ones, bringing new and different ways to do things. Paradigms are significant because they limit us and stifle our willingness to change. And remember, if we aren't willing to change, we can't grow. Paradigms help us decide good from bad, right from wrong, "should I" from "shouldn't I." They are the boundaries, the fences by which we encircle ourselves. We choose whether to accept new information or to keep it out. Thus, our paradigms create our *screenery*—our self-satisfied view of things. Our screenery is our way of staying happy with complacency. Unless we get close to our fences, we won't come near identifying what we need to change.

* * * * *

In 1968, Swiss watchmakers controlled 90 percent of the wealth in that industry. Advertisements emphasized the twenty-one jewels and other aesthetic or mechanical advantages used in the manufacture of the conventional movement watch. Then along came electronics and the quartz movement, and the use of bearings, springs and gears became obsolete. The Swiss invented this new technology but ignored its great potential. Unfortunately, the Swiss watchmakers were blinded by the screenery of the investment they had made in the old way. Along came Seiko of Japan and, as they say, "the rest is history."

* * * * *

Likewise, computer aided design (CAD) systems came along and totally changed the way draftsmen work today. Hey, remember slide rules? That was an incredible business before someone came up with electronic calculators. Did you ever hear of carbon paper? I bet your grandchild won't! It was an essential office supply before we had photocopy machines.

* * * * *

Chester Carlson came along with a whole new way of photographing things. He went to a major photographic company and said, "Look what happens when you do this with a sensitized plate—you get this image." They threw him out, exclaiming that was no way to make pictures! Ah, but Carlson had the last laugh. He had invented the Xerox™ process. They said it couldn't be done. Now what would an office be like—what would the world be like—without photocopiers?

* * * * *

We recently experienced the colossal act of going back to zero in an old paradigm called the U.S.S.R. (Union of Soviet Socialist Republics—Russia). Here we were building heat-seeking cruise missiles to go down chimneys and search out the enemy because of this large evil empire that was after us. Now it has crumbled and we have to change our own country's focus as a result.

* * * * *

In these terms, "paradigm paralysis" is synonymous with inflexibility. Bernie Fields, Dick Hadel and Hy Fink were paradigm pioneers to me. They certainly showed me there is no such thing as "you can't." I met them when I was quite young and they were in the retail business. Back in the 1950s, who would have wanted to buy basket chairs from Hong Kong, Philippine mahogany plywood, Italian glass clowns, Hawaiian ferns or binoculars from Japan? This trio spent $13,000 in 1957 for a full-page ad in the *Los Angeles Times* to attract people to their sheet-metal retail store. Ultimately, their business became a very large department store chain that was later purchased by Thrifty Drug Stores.

We must stimulate our own change so we can remain in control of our future. Identifying our current paradigms and changing our direction is essential. Then we will be more successful by *our* definition. Increased efficiency and happiness follow.

*"We need to recognize the tremendous power which lies in all of us and which we cannot use as long as we feel victimized."*

—Rudolf Dreikurs

# Chapter Eleven
# I Found the Enemy–Thanks, Oprah

Oprah Winfrey is to be admired for having worked hard to achieve a successful career with accompanying wealth. Through her television forum, she has raised the level of awareness for life's atrocities and abuses. Whether it be between husband and wife, child and parent or friend and friend, she has elevated that stream of consciousness regarding human relationships.

All of us, to varying degrees, have had terrible things happen to us that we could use, very conveniently, as the reason we're not where we would like to be or could be. Unfortunately, using such reasons as excuses is counterproductive from a personal growth standpoint.

In interviewing principals within companies, I hear many stories about why people do not achieve their dreams. There was a time when we mainly heard that a person didn't get the proper education or didn't have the right opportunities to overcome adversity.

Now Geraldo, Maury and Ricki have given us a forum for commiserating about our miseries and talking about our shortcomings and the terrible things that have happened to us. The format justifies excuses and exploits people's agonies. The result is we're given even bigger and better alibis for not reaching our goals. However, such exercises eradicate the thought that we have a future. People enjoy these shows, and the producers of them capitalize on that fact to sell advertising.

The past cannot be changed. Our parents were not perfect, life is not perfect and our relationships are not perfect.

Our previous actions and the previous actions of others are the only things that cannot be changed. We have yet, however, to shape the future. If we put our energies to proactive use, we will invent the future, our future. And as far as our pasts, and especially our parents, are concerned, as Frank Pitman, whom I admire very much, says, "It takes a pretty inept child to require perfect parents."

*"The fault, dear Brutus,*
*is not in our stars*
*but in ourselves...."*

—William Shakespeare

# Part III
# You Mean It's My Fault?

An ambitious young man by the name of Kirk was hired by a company that used a variety of chemicals to coat metals. The company's name was Abbotwares. Kirk's job was to take unfinished parts and polish them on a polishing machine in preparation for their coating in another location. Because the job was so tedious, he tried to figure out ways to make the task more important and exciting. Kirk was surrounded by people with negative attitudes. One blamed the coating wheel for malfunctioning and making it necessary for him to apply more rouge to it constantly. Art, the foreman, was fond of pitting workers against each other with words like "How come he can do more than you can do?"

Another fellow exclaimed, "They seem to be giving me all the bad parts. Jake gets all the good ones; I get the bad ones." Whatever happened in that plant, it was always the fault of some other person or of the equipment.

But Kirk rose above all the negativity and created a positive attitude that infected the rest of the group:

First he started to whistle, hum and even sing. He wore a smile and thought of the things he was going to learn, continuing to nourish his feeling of significance in the processes that were all around him.

He clearly defined what he was doing and how he could make it better and more productive. He set a challenging but achievable productivity standard for the number of the various parts he would polish. He developed a game based on beating his old record of parts per hour. Frequently rearranging the physical organization of his work station and constantly thinking of how he could make it better, he would break his old record and feel good about it, sharing his jubilation with his fellow workers and Art.

Because polishing constantly with his right hand in control made that hand and arm become fatigued, he experimented with switching hands and found that alternately resting one hand maintained his constant output. He was having fun and everyone knew it. He found quicker ways to rouge the wheel and transfer finished and unfinished parts, and he managed to eliminate some of the so-called "best and only ways" to do things.

After three weeks had passed, he was visited by the big boss, Sam Lippert. Sam said, "I've noticed that you're doing a great job, and I'm increasing your hourly pay 5 cents to 60 cents per hour. Do you think you can show the others how to do as well as you?"

Kirk was 16 years old and this was a summer job. By the time school started he had learned to run an engine lathe and gold-, nickel-, zinc- and copperplate metal parts. Mastering how to keep the plating tanks functional and the chemical solution properly mixed earned him the respect and admiration of the majority of the staff. When it was time to go back to school the most significant thing he had accomplished was a dramatic improvement in the attitude of his fellow employees, which resulted in a much better place to work. And by the way, through the rest of high school and during part of college he always had a home and a job at Abbotwares. He especially enjoyed the many productive relationships he developed.

All the preceding is a true story. I know Kirk and knew the big boss, Sam, well. Kirk is a very successful businessman who has had many successes in his journey through life and is still having a lot of fun. No surprise!

* * * * *

Jerry worked on an order desk along with sixty other people, taking orders over the phone. When the supervisor measured Jerry's productivity against the other workers on the phone desk, his figures fell far below. "Yeah," Jerry piped up, "but I have all the difficult customers, and I take all the hard orders."

The supervisor rebuffed Jerry's comments. "Uh-huh, we answer the phone with the company name, thank the person for calling, and then ask, 'Is this going to be an easy order or a difficult request?' If they reply that the order will take time and will be difficult to fill, then we give the call to you, Jerry. Now, let's talk about what we can do to get your productivity figures increased to be in line with the others."

Jerry got the message. Although he had to work hard and struggle, slowly but surely his productivity and attitude improved. He occasionally would fall back into his old ways, but he would always pick himself up, mostly on his own. He began actively emulating the better performers and developing pride first in himself and then as part of the team.

* * * * *

Who is responsible when things don't go the way we want them to? Who has the ultimate control over our future? Who are we blaming? Who are we holding accountable? We cheat ourselves anytime we blame anything on someone else.

*"The only way I can be completely stress-free is to be completely dead—not a very inviting choice!"*

—James Straub

# Chapter Twelve When Am I done and When Will I Get There?

Change, change, change. It never stops. When is it going to be done? Is it soup yet? When do I get there? Hopefully never, because *there* is the end of the journey. All living things are either growing or they're dying. And when people say, "I hate getting old," one has to believe they're not considering the alternative!

When you go on a shopping spree, are you amazed at how things have been moved and displays relocated since the last time you were in the store? You know such rearrangements are planned to help move merchandise, but it can be frustrating when you're searching for that perfect scarf for Aunt Mabel that you intended to get on your last visit. Still, you would be disappointed if you went into the shop more than twice and didn't find new and different items just tempting you to part with your money.

Despite our reluctance, we desire variety, at least in our shopping! Change must be embraced as an adventure so that we're too challenged to want it to end.

*****

At the age of forty-eight I undertook such an adventure when I started my own business. I left a comfortable, well-paying position to the cries of "You can't!" because I wanted to have more fun—which I always insist upon—and because I wanted to continue to grow. I decided to become a management consultant so I could help companies by sharing the knowledge I've gained through my experiences. I had clients from day one, and some of them are still with me.

In this consulting process, it became apparent to me that I needed to continue to grow. So I became involved in the brokerage business—the buying, selling, merging and valuating of companies. I also developed my own seminars first and then became licensed to do workshops and seminars for others. One of my oldest alliances is with Personal Awareness Systems, Inc., headquartered in Sausalito, California. It was one of the first companies to undertake social-style profiling along with its hypothesized underlying genetic encoding.

My almost immediate success in consulting led to another change: I branched out to become a general management consultant. I didn't specialize in any industry but generalized in every industry and didn't specialize at any level but knew from the beginning that I would need to work from the top level of management down. With continued success, I found that suddenly my competitors wanted to join forces. So I made another change: I joined a company called Management Action Programs and soon became one of its principals and a stockholder.

Yet change beckoned again in 1991 when I sold the stock and once more went out on my own with a new paradigm and started to refer to myself as a "futurist." I broke away from traditional general management consulting and formed my own company called Persona Management Consulting Group, Inc. My emphasis now is on discovering or inventing the future and spending time with a variety of other approaches including strategic planning, strategic alliances and various kinds of presentations. Now I rely more on intuition and less on penciling, more on inventing and self-fulfilling and less on managing and monitoring.

These continual changes have led me through continued growth, self-improvement, reinvention of the future and, most important, increased self-accountability. Be open to change and watch your future unfold as well!

*"It is a bad plan*
*that cannot be changed."*

—Publilius Syrus

*"If we do not change our direction,*
*we are likely to end up*
*where we are headed."*

—Chinese proverb

# Chapter Thirteen
# I Have a Plan?

There is a reason for the question mark in this chapter title. If we ask someone whether they have a plan for achieving their goals, they will reply, "Of course." (The person is thinking, "If I give a pat answer quickly, they will stop these questions," and is secretly hoping no one will ask for details on the plan.) As long as the question requires only a yes or a no answer, no further explanation is needed. Uh-huh, uh-huh, that's the way we like it. And, if we didn't have to make a plan more than once in our lives, we'd be in absolute hog heaven!

To many people, the ultimate in planning goes something like "Shove me out the door in the morning, stuff me in my car, drive me to work, let me put up with my boss for eight hours and then shovel me home. Whew, I made it! Plan implemented."

Do you notice how many more people are being honored by weatherman Willard Scott on "The Today

Show" for reaching their hundredth birthdays or beyond—even within the past year? Some statistics being introduced now indicate that the majority of people will still have 33 percent of their lives to live after age fifty. So, you'd better forget about that rocking chair on the front porch. You'll soon be quite bored with that lifestyle if you don't have some ideas on how you're going to be spending your time.

A real plan requires a clear destination and a clearly defined journey:

1. Here's where I have been.
2. Here's where I am.
3. Here's where I am going.
4. Here's how I am going to get there.
5. Here's when I am going to get there.

You alone can determine whether you're a passenger on the ship of life's journey or you're at the helm, guiding the voyage. Time is our most precious resource, yet we expend far more energy planning how we'll spend our money than how we'll utilize our time. Robert A. Heinlein writes, "Time is your total capital and the minutes of your life are painfully few.... So learn to say no.... Otherwise, you will not have time to carry out your duty or to do your own work, and certainly no time for love or happiness." This is so true!

Take a piece of paper and list everything you do. Identify which of these activities are the most significant and give them a priority number. You may be surprised at some of the ways you waste your time and wonder why you do some things at all. Some activities probably will be on the list simply because you enjoy doing them. Others will be left off the list. These are probably the most important ones and they need to be done, but they get sacrificed because you see them as being unpleasant or too difficult to do. Setting priorities is very simple and very basic. As John Wooden, the famous basketball coach has stated on the essentials of that game, "Dribble, pass, shoot."

With all the products like Day-Timer™, preprinted blank "Things to Do Today" lists and electronic pocket calendars, there's no reason we can't list items to be completed on a daily basis, along with a numbering system to prioritize each item. Time management is most important. Take control of your life or someone else will. "Define or be defined."

*"Things which matter most*
*must never be at the mercy*
*of things which matter least."*

—Goethe

# Chapter Fourteen
# The Pareto Principle—Taking the "Trivial Many" and Narrowing Them Down to the "Vital Few"

The nineteenth century Italian economist Wilfredo Pareto gave us the 80/20 rule: 80 percent of the wealth belongs to 20 percent of the people. In business, this rule applies as a general constant. Twenty percent of the items sold represent 80 percent of total sales. Twenty percent of the clients represent 80 percent of the business. Twenty percent of a company's personnel represent 80 percent of the company's problems. Pareto also gave us two very useful phrases: the *trivial many,* which refers to the vast number of matters that are truly unimportant but that have a tendency to bog us down; and the *vital few,* which are the items we need to concentrate on but tend to shove aside while we attempt to satisfy the trivial many.

On your list of priorities, out of ten items, only two usually need to be done. The other eight either don't need to be done at all, don't need to be done by you or don't need to be done as often as you're doing them. At the end of the day, we measure how hard we've worked by how tired we are, as opposed to whether we accomplished the vital few and disposed of, bypassed or ignored the trivial many.

I once worked with someone who considered everything to be top priority. It was not unusual for this individual to have four or five inches of solid paper on the top of the desk. You could pick up some of the dated pieces, though, and see that they had been published as much as ten months earlier. Apparently, he was hanging onto them because he didn't know how to deal with them, or didn't want to. But as long as they were on his desk, he felt very busy and important because he had so much to do. He took great joy in the trivial many.

Government bureaucracy, as most know, is greatly infected with the trivial many. Department after department deals in nothing but detail on how to accomplish the larger task. There are reports, placed in binders, that no one ever sees. At one time, those reports were thought to contain good ideas. And each of those reports was one of someone's vital few items to perform before being able to go home on a particular evening.

But let's not kid ourselves. Private enterprise, too, is laden with too many meetings, reports, memos and lengthy feasibility studies. I know of at least one company that has found the solution to lengthy meetings. The management has removed all the chairs from the conference room! It's amazing how much shorter and productive those meetings have become, now that no one can get comfortable sitting in those overstuffed chairs.

So what can we do? Consider the following suggestions:

1. Communicate priorities, giving everyone a chance to participate in the process.
2. No agenda, no meeting.
3. Develop mission statements—for the company, your department, yourself.
4. Involve everyone in setting meaningful goals in harmony with your mission.
5. Utilize all of your resources in relation to your goals.
6. Initiate being prepared and stamp out the trivia.
7. Assign tasks and hold yourself and others accountable.
8. Follow up and follow through.
9. Align yourself and, if applicable, your organization to the vision and mission.
10. And most importantly, get "buy-in" and adherence to these rules from those participating.

*"Never tell people how to do things.*
*Tell them what to do,*
*and they will surprise you*
*with their ingenuity."*

—George S. Patton

# Chapter Fifteen How Delegation and Empowerment Fit In

We say we don't delegate because:

1. We are convinced no one can do it as well as we can.
2. By the time we explain it, we could have done it ourselves.
3. It might not get done if we give it to someone else to do.

Actually, we don't delegate because we really enjoy doing it ourselves. We enjoy being so good at something that nobody else can do (because we've never given them a chance to learn how to do it), and if we don't do it, we might have to do something we're not comfortable doing. What we're missing out on is that delegating stimulates self-accountability in others, so everybody wins.

Some wit said, "If you always do what you've always done, you'll always get what you've always got." And typically, we do the same things over and over again, working harder each time, but expecting different results—a pretty good definition of insanity! Perhaps someone else could bring a fresh approach to the situation and do it better. Maybe if we take the time to explain it once, we'll have helped train someone to do it in the future. If we empower others, they'll get it done, and we'll have time to focus on our "vital few" list.

A strong leader knows how to get things done through delegation. Entrusting responsibility stimulates self-accountability in others by stating the desired result and allowing room for their ingenuity—which in turn instills self-confidence and increased skills.

Regarding delegation, Booker T. Washington said, "Few things help an individual more than for another to place responsibility upon him, and to let him know that he is trusted."

*"The best way out is through."*

—Helen Keller

# Chapter Sixteen
# Sing It All the Way Through

We all know that worry is the biggest waste of our time and energy. Worry does not change circumstances. We can imagine the worst situations and fret ourselves to death, but that still will not change the outcome.

Mothers seem especially prone to develop this trait. It's ironic that they rear their children to become mature and independent, yet as soon as the fledglings move out of the house, they begin wishing that Bobby or Susie hadn't taken the wonderful job opportunity that required a move to another city (even though the position means financial independence). These parents are certain that their grown children are spending way too much money for rent but not nearly enough on the right kind of food to maintain their minimum daily requirement of riboflavin!

A current commercial portrays a son/husband

taking incoming long-distance phone calls from first his mother and then his wife. In both instances, he must assure them he's eating quite well, since neither one is in town to personally oversee his diet. All the time he's talking with them, he's nibbling on a slice of pizza. While it's true that pizza is considered to be one of the healthier fast food offerings, it still doesn't contain all the essential food groups in one sitting. They can worry all they want, but their concern will not magically replace that pizza slice with a low-fat meal loaded with vitamins, minerals and antioxidants.

Worrying, as a hobby, replaces reason. But if you ask a worrier to tell you what is first and foremost on their fret list, that person will blurt out, "I don't know."

* * * * *

Remember the countless times you've started singing a song or whistling a tune and you kept repeating it all day long? Do you want to get rid of it? Sing it once, all the way through. It will go away.

Singing the "worry" song all the way through requires that you sit down with a pen and paper and answer the question: "What in my life is important?" If you take the time to prioritize a list, you'll probably discover that things are in much better shape than they seemed before your analysis. At the very least, you'll discover exactly what to worry about rather than just worrying about worrying.

Take a moment to think a situation all the way through. You'll find that it's not nearly so bad as you first might have thought. Ask yourself: What's the worst thing that could happen? Listen carefully to the answer. Decide how much sense it makes to maintain this state of worry.

*"I find that the great thing in this world is not so much where we stand, as is what direction we are moving."*

—Oliver Wendell Holmes

# Chapter Seventeen
# The Recipe

Goals equal results. The following list contains the ingredients for outlining personal growth goals:

1. Stay committed. Focus on the vital few.
2. State each goal as a positive statement: "I will..."
3. Establish personally rewarding goals.
4. Formulate goals that stimulate personal commitment.
5. Set goals that enhance relationships.
6. Ensure that achievement of goals demonstrates identifiable change.
7. Challenge yourself to stretch beyond your comfort zone and break through your screenery.

In all kinds of settings, whether they be job interviews, counseling sessions, yearly reviews or quarterly financial statements, assess your strengths and weaknesses. Ask for and analyze feedback from others, and then sort out your strengths and weaknesses again. The whole process is similar to separating the cream from the milk, the wheat from the chaff. What comes out at the top of the list are the vital few. There will be some pain involved in this process because it forces us to step outside our comfort zones, but it'll be worth it.

In assessment of strengths and weaknesses, you can only look at the 10 percent that are visible—those qualities that you choose to allow others to see. No one can examine your brain, go into your heart or dig deep to get your gut reactions. So all anyone has to go on are your answers to silent questions such as "Do you smile or not?" When the boss walks in the door, employees know whether they want to stay away because of the aura that individual is emanating. And people use that perception all the time to avoid change. They'll say, "That's just the way people think I am." My songwriting psychologist friend Carroll Thomas calls that Popeyeism—"I yam what I yam!"

In my workshops, when participants hear feedback from their peers stating that they're "self-centered" and "condescending" or that they "don't care about people," their initial reaction is usually "That's just the way people think I am. I'm not really that way." Well, yes, they really are that way since "perception is reality." The real "you" is always showing, whether you want to believe it or not, even though we all want to be on the side of the angels.

Individuals are endowed with many strengths,

but they never run out of weaknesses either. However, those weaknesses are not easily identifiable by oneself, because they require great objectivity. Our self-guardian—or self-regarding— mechanisms don't allow us to view our own drawbacks. "I guess it would be to my advantage to be a bit more expansive and expressive, but gee, I'm just not comfortable being that way."

Enlist one or more of your confidants and ask each of them to tell you about yourself. Pay attention to what others say about you, judgmental or not. Their perceptions are likely to be more accurate than your perception of yourself. Build on your apparent weaknesses that they are kind enough to tell you about and turn them into strengths.

*"Even if you are on the right track,*
*you'll get run over*
*if you just sit there."*

—Will Rogers

# Chapter Eighteen Setting Standards, Assessing Performance and Taking Self-Corrective Action

Stay organized. For those who want to be like Martha Stewart, juggling fifteen projects at one time, supervising the addition of an east wing to the house, planting the entire vegetable garden in one day, making candles for this evening's dinner party and showing up at the door to greet guests looking "mah-vel-ous" while carrying on scintillating conversation with every single person present, this chapter is for you. How do we keep ourselves on track? How do we know we're moving at the appropriate pace?

We need to set standards, assess performance and take corrective action with people who work for us, and we also need to do all these same things for ourselves. When you assess your own performance, you must be honest with yourself and that means involving others in the process.

Positioning yourself with a confidant is an integral part of the growth process. To whom do you turn? Professionally, psychologists are confidants. Ministers are confidants. But in the circle of people that you know, there are probably several friends about whom you feel good and whom you trust. They will be wonderful resources for you, especially if they're honest and objective and have no negative ulterior motives.

Your confidants should have nothing to gain if you backslide; they succeed only if you succeed. Objectivity is key in this role. They should harbor no hidden agendas or vested interests in you or in what you are trying to accomplish. These confidants will assist you in identifying whether or not you're achieving your personal goals and objectives.

"I did it! I finally accomplished the goal of getting the bachelor's degree I've been working on for the past seven years by going to school part time and working full time!"

Once you achieve one goal, you can set another and achieve that one. You naturally put your shoulders back, jut your chin out and walk with a new confidence. Believe it—you almost literally start growing taller. It just simply feels good. Whatever your goal is, to set it and achieve it is as contagious as it is exhilarating. As a result, others will also want to try harder to make their own dreams come true. You will find yourself surrounded by people achieving their dreams and sharing in each other's happiness.

*"For a person not to know that he has an inferiority complex, and how to use it, is like going through life in poverty, not knowing that someone has left you a million dollars."*

—Marie Beynon Ray

# Chapter Nineteen
# Look Out, Complacency!

How can insecurity assist me in achieving my personal growth goals?

Our plan of action needs to include equal and necessary doses of "positive insecurity." This sounds like an oxymoron, and it is. But, paradoxical as it seems, insecurity can serve as a great motivator, a catalyst. We want to be sure that we're constantly challenging ourselves to move in and out of the wobblies to keep ourselves from becoming complacent. Remember: no wobblies, no growth; no growth means stagnation. Growth and change become our self-initiated self-esteem builders. Even the psychiatric profession has come to think that it might be preferable to have their patients feel somewhat less than totally comfortable.

Presidents of companies who attend my seminars often express the wish to go back to the days when they had fewer employees. They feel they were far more profitable and experienced far fewer problems.

They feel morale was better and teamwork was greater. However, companies that choose to limit growth will experience eventual demise.

Public speakers, actors and musicians usually admit that butterflies in the stomach are standard operating procedure before a speech or performance. In fact, the absence of such emotion is very rare. When complacency sets in, the edge disappears and the presentation is less than inspired—and less inspiring!

Being frightened is a natural feeling. It's part of the job, performers will tell you, and that is utterly correct. However, once these same people begin to speak or to perform, their nerves settle down and they become enraptured. The audience is in store for a delightfully memorable experience.

*"What kind of man would live*
*where there is no daring?*
*I don't believe in taking foolish chances.*
*But nothing can be accomplished*
*without taking any chance at all."*

—Charles A. Lindberg

# Part IV
# Can I Learn This?

We will embrace the process and continue the journey. In so doing, we will learn the basis for all personal growth opportunity—self-accountability.

*"All we have to do is keep our eye on the target.*
*Obstacles are those frightening things*
*you see when you take your eye off the target."*
—Curtis L. Carlson

So how are we going to get there? What are the guidelines for the actions to be taken? Keep in mind that if a genie popped out of a bottle at this moment, it would be important to know what you would wish for.

A well-thought-out strategic plan will contain the following critical elements:

1. an established relationship with one or more confidants (identify and align yourself with someone

else who is already successful at what it is you want to accomplish);

2. the use of strengths to achieve your goals;

3. the transmutation of weaknesses into strengths.

Remember, your confidants must be objective. They may even change from time to time. Identify with success examples so you can watch and be inspired by people who are doing what you're trying to accomplish and doing it well. Identify and use your strengths as tools in the growth process. Turn your weaknesses into strengths. Constantly solicit other people's input. Be prepared to adopt a new lifestyle. Use experience and knowledge as a channel for change rather than as a barrier. Be accountable to yourself and to your higher purpose.

*"Dreams are seedlings of realities."*

—James Allen

*"A rockpile ceases to be a rockpile*
*the moment a single man*
*contemplates it, bearing within him*
*the image of a cathedral."*

—Antoine de Saint-Exupery

# Chapter Twenty
# Dreams, Vision and the Journey

Every significant occurrence in our life starts out as a dream. We need to listen to our dreams. Most important, we must put action to our dreams. Dreams plus action equal vision. Dreams in action are the stuff that change the entire world. Action, without dreams, simply passes time.

Historians are quick to point out that preceding every great event in the history of mankind, there are dreams detailing what is to come. We need to develop these dreams by putting action to them.

*"To accomplish great things,*
*we must not only act but also dream,*
*not only plan but also believe."*
—Anatole France

Bruce's Layne's father died when he was young, leaving Bruce with the responsibility of helping to support his mother and brother. He worked his way through college on a partial athletic scholarship in baseball. He worked very hard to learn the insurance agency business and had the courage to start his own agency approximately eighteen years ago.

Recently, I had the pleasure of being involved in his political campaign as he ran for lieutenant governor of the state of Nevada. He is one who gives back to his community in return for the many times he was helped as a young man. Obviously, he overcame great adversity and is a tribute to the result of working on dreams and putting them into action. He is a very happy, family-oriented, spiritual man.

* * * * *

Things that are hard are the only things worth doing. If they are easy, you've already done them. True success is the journey itself. If it were only the destination, then what would follow? Life's journey is filled with precious moments and opportunities that we entertain to make it all worthwhile. Once again we all need to hold ourselves accountable if we are not making this happen for us.

*"There is no record of any individual making a truly great contribution to civilization without the cooperation of others."*

—Napoleon Hill

# Chapter Twenty-One
# Talking to People Who Have Been Around

The more you surround yourself with people who hold you accountable, the more they will bring out the ability in you to think and act like you can do anything and make anything happen.

People are all just people. Whether someone is the president of a major corporation or your next-door neighbor, that person feels and breathes like you do. Listen to the people around you. You'll understand yourself a little better and you won't feel so badly about your own fallibility. Pay particular attention to those who are successful. What you will find is that they're almost completely self-accountable.

* * * * *

Joe and Neil were two young men who soon after graduating from high school, decided to start their own business rather than working for someone else. They were determined to make it without assistance from others. Each was distinctly individual and possessed different motivators, but they were both determined to be successful in their own way and their own style. Through teamwork they attained their goal of putting together a very successful promotions company, Schmidt-Cannon. Joe, the sales-oriented promoter, and Neil, the results-oriented administrator, complement each other perfectly.

The pair set up shop under the stairwell at the Sears Roebuck & Co. store in La Puente, California, and simply offered a free gold-plated chain necklace to anyone who applied for a Sears charge card. In spite of the fact that they had no encouragement from any outside source, Joe and Neil built a business that grew to international dimensions. They were the cover story in *Inc.* magazine a few years ago, and in the article they described the pitfalls they experienced on the journey to success and how they used their relationship to the greatest advantage.

* * * * *

You can learn from people you have never even met; these role models are invariably people who emphasize the things they have been able to do rather than the things they have not been able to do. You can make yourself increasingly self-accountable by actively seeking out examples like this. And it can be just plain fun.

*"We are all salespeople....*
*Everybody is selling something—*
*an idea, a dream, or a point of view."*

—W. Clement Stone

# Chapter Twenty-Two
# Self Promotion: Selling Yourself to Yourself

The word *selling* is viewed by many as a dirty word. Selling is something that about half the world is less than excited about. It brings to mind the stereotypical obnoxious, unscrupulous car salesperson.

That's not what selling is about. It's not a facade. Selling is genuinely articulating your ideas and the things you would like to see yourself and others accomplish. The message becomes so enticing that others want to become part of that process, and they feel good about doing it. Sales, appropriately defined, becomes both an art form and a science. We're all in sales because we all have to learn to sell ourselves.

Most children are taught not to boast about their achievements, and this can cause problems. It can set the stage for low self-esteem. As adults, if you can't sell yourself to yourself, you're not likely to be able to sell yourself to anyone else. Be honest with yourself about how truly important and significant you are to yourself and feel good about it. Sell to yourself all those marvelous dreams you're going to put into action and then sell yourself on putting them into action. Most important, sell yourself on being accountable when your dreams don't happen as quickly as you would like.

If you want to be successful, visualize being successful and picture yourself in that position—act as if you are successful. Such visualization has tremendous value. If there's something about the way you dress or about your physical appearance that friends have told you would be better if it were changed, and it can be modified, heed that advice. Sometimes a change in hairstyle or buying new clothes can make a tremendous difference in how you're seen by others. This is especially true if you sense you're being held back in what you can accomplish.

* * * * *

I recently met someone who was not happy about his job title. He was listed as the assistant general manager, and he wanted very much to be the vice-president and general manager. I encouraged him to begin acting like a vice-president and general manager. Guess what? He is now the vice-president and general manager. "Look like who you want to be—and that's who you'll become."

You can sell anything to anyone when you can sell yourself to yourself. Get comfortable being a self-promoter, even though it may seem distasteful at first. Consider other people and their dreams, ambitions and interests as well, and this can become quite a delicious dish indeed.

*"You manage things.*
*You lead people."*

—Admiral Grace Hooper

# Chapter Twenty-Three
# Stimulating Self-Motivation That Is Self-Leadership

Managers have become obsolete in favor of leaders. Leaders, by definition, are people who can stimulate self-motivation in other people. A true leader does not motivate but stimulates self-motivation.

In relationships, we need to hold ourselves accountable to each other to stimulate self-motivation. We must surround ourselves with people who provide this stimulation.

We have no idea what we're each capable of doing. We need to lead ourselves to all those great things we're going to do. Some companies, however, are happy maintaining the status quo. They're fond of saying, "This is the way my father did it. This is the way it's going to be done." I am aware of a corporation (if they are still in business) that produces twelve copies of hand-typed invoices. They could be making a major contribution because they have an incredible product line and some very talented people whom they hold back. However, the owners subscribe to a philosophy of management rather than to a self- and other-motivating notion of leadership.

At the time I consulted with this company, we were preparing to install some very basic computer technology. But we ran into all kinds of resistance such as "The day you put a computer in my office is the day we shut this place down." This kind of organization ensures that employee lunch is always at 11:30 a.m. Management is more concerned about playing a game of Hearts at the break than finding better ways of purchasing products, warehousing and stocking material or entering orders. Believe it or not, at the time I was doing business with them, they still used straight pins rather than staples and considered carbon paper a preferable alternative to installing a copy machine. These kinds of people are all around us, and their screenery is my greatest challenge.

These are the ones who are sent to my workshops not because they want to attend but because their superiors want them to grow. Usually, their initial comments are something like "I've been in this business for twenty-seven years." "I've forgotten more about this business than my boss will ever know." "We're not doing anything wrong, and everything's just fine." "It's just some people's imagination that teamwork doesn't exist, that morale is bad or that we don't communicate."

And I'm thinking, "The reason business is falling off is because they haven't done anything new or creative for the past five years. They don't want to because they're comfortable with the way things are." These employees can come to work in the morning half-awake, sleepwalk through most of the day, put in their eight hours and snooze home.

I try to help these individuals realize how much more satisfying their jobs would be if they became more self-accountable, accepting both the credit and the blame.

Most people have no idea what they're truly capable of doing. We all had best lead ourselves and others to all the great things we were created to do.

*"Different, but equal,*
*is the only answer."*

—Marie Beynon Ray

# Chapter Twenty-Four
# A Lesson in Style

I am a student and strong advocate of the science of social style profiling. I practice it, as do millions of people throughout the world, some more deliberately than others. I have also taught this science to hundreds of other people.

Social style profiling is a simple science to learn; it began in the 1950s when Dr. Charles Osgood started doing what turned out to be massive research on how different people see people differently. These differences cause us to react differently to different people. Being different is good. However, we tend to get along best with the people who are most like ourselves. Our tendency is to miscommunicate with people and have difficulty developing trust with people who have been genetically encoded with one of the other three social styles. Even though there is no right or wrong or good or bad social style, we tend to regard people with social styles different from our own as difficult to deal with.

In order to continually improve our people skills—and since communication is at least 80 percent of our people skills—I recommend we learn more about the differences in people and how we are perceived by others. As you have now learned, the only person you can change is yourself, and it's your responsibility to convey meaning and obtain understanding. This doesn't mean changing your genetic social style, but rather simply approaching people in a manner that satisfies and respects their needs and creates a win-win situation.

Here is how simple it is:

Everyone falls somewhere on two scales, one represented by a horizontal line the other by a vertical line. Take a piece of paper or picture a line running horizontally across the middle of your paper from left to right. At the extreme left end, write the word *dominant* and at the extreme right end the word *unassuming*. Assign a scale of 1 to 10 with equal gradations and with the value of 1 at the right side where you have written *unassuming*. Assign the value 10 to the *dominant* end. Using characteristics you associate with these two words in conjunction with the characteristics described on the following pages for dominant and unassuming, place the letter Y (for you) where you believe you fall on this scale. You may also place an O (other person) where you think a person with whom you have difficulty communicating would fall.

Now draw a vertical line that dissects the

horizontal line at its midpoint or 5. At the top of this line write the word *expansive* and at the bottom, *contained*. Gradate the vertical line from 1 to 10, placing the 1 at *contained* end and the 10 at the *expansive* end. Where do you fall on this scale? Using your own definitions and those that follow, place a Y at that point and an O where that same difficult person would fall.

You now have created a quadrant of four squares. Going clockwise beginning at the upper left quadrant, 1 = dominant expansive, 2 = unassuming expansive, 3 = unassuming contained and 4 = dominant contained.

Connect your two Y's ( the horizontal one and the vertical one) going into the square where they meet and do the same for your two O's. You and the other person fall in one of these four squares. Various words can be used to label these squares, but I prefer to classify them according to four social styles. Dominant expansive people fall under the *promoting* social style; unassuming expansive, *facilitating* social style; unassuming contained, *analytical* social style; and dominant contained, *controlling* social style.

These are their basic needs:

- The promoting social style seeks recognition.
- The facilitating social style seeks acceptance.
- The analytical social style seeks security.
- The controlling social style seeks achievement.

If you have done the exercise, I predict that you are likely to be in an opposite quadrant from your other person (the one you may be having difficulty with). This can and usually does create a challenge for both of you.

There exist computer tools to do this exercise most effectively, knowing now that others' perceptions are reality, you would have five objective people who know you well fill out a questionnaire. These are available from Persona®, Personal Awareness Systems, Inc. A computer analysis of the questionnaires would reveal your social style, degree of empathy and degree of flexibility, all the elements that go into developing better lines of open communication and building productive relationships.

*Dominant* people tend to be talkative, confident and controlling and to make statements that are direct and challenging. They're usually assertive, aggressive people who make good suggestions—and they have plenty of suggestions too! They tend to interrupt a lot.

*Unassuming* folks tend to be quiet and uncertain and usually ask a lot of questions. They also are facilitating. They aren't so direct; they're usually subtle and gentle, and they're very good listeners.

So what we have here is a one-line decision we unwittingly make when we meet somebody. Is this person telling me what to do or am I able to tell him or her what to do? Is this person making statements or asking questions? Is he or she pushy or passive? We're asking ourselves these things without even thinking about it.

We're also asking ourselves a second question. Where on a continuum between expansive and contained do these individuals fit? Are these people *expansive*, promoting, open, warm and expressive, or are they *contained*, analytical, cool and rigid? Fortunately, there is no right or wrong, good or bad. Every one of us falls somewhere into one of the four quadrants to a great degree with a bit of the other three quadrants' characteristics.

*"Do unto others as they would want you to do unto them."*

—Al Marino

# Chapter Twenty-Five
# Maybe Not Wrong, just Different

In order to better identify and understand the different social styles, it may be useful to relate each style to popular TV and movie detective characters. An example of the *expansive, dominant* (promoting) social style is Magnum, P.I., with his flair, openness, warmth and expression of emotion—driving around in his expensive foreign car!

The *expansive, unassuming* (facilitating) social style characteristics are evident in the character of Colombo, who appears to be extremely concerned about avoiding confrontation and to seek an open exchange of information. He wants to win acceptance, tries hard not to say things people don't want to hear and doesn't want to inconvenience anyone in any way.

The famous Charlie Chan is more obviously into the detail of it all and concentrates on being very thorough with all the information available to solve the crime. There's very little concentration on feelings, his or others, with focus on the facts in great precision—characteristic of the *unassuming, contained* (analytical) social style.

Sergeant Joe Friday of *Dragnet* typifies the *contained, dominant* (controlling) social style. He wants "just the facts, ma'am," with little or no embellishment. And, as with Charlie Chan, feelings are of no significance.

* * * * *

We're all familiar with the Golden Rule: "Do unto others as you would have them do unto you." When developing productive relationships, this rule, as stated, works only about 25 percent of the time. Therefore, 75 percent of the time we're going to fall flat on our faces. I would suggest an alternative rule—a different paradigm: "Do unto others as they would want you to do unto them." In other words, talk to other people the way they want to be talked to rather than the way we ourselves want to be talked to.

For better communication, we would be wise to appeal to a people's individual tastes—their greatest preferences. For, as the Latin saying goes, "In matters of tastes, there's no dispute." People are different, and that's not only okay, it's good. Can you imagine how boring things would be if people were all the same? Most of us tend to be judgmental of other people's social styles, however, if they're different from our own. But different is not wrong. Even if it were, as Paul Hauck says, "People have the right to be wrong!" Don't prejudge people—that's called prejudice!

It comes down to basics. Eighty-five percent of our effectiveness in most areas of life is dependent upon how well we communicate. Thus, we benefit from reminding ourselves that it's our responsibility to communicate well. We had best take ownership of being able to convey meaning effectively and to obtain understanding.

Building productive relationships is about building trust. That trust will be based on

- what you say and do
- what you don't say and do
- the way you act

It will not be based on

- your thoughts and feelings
- your values, priorities and needs

These qualities may be invisible to the person with whom you're communicating. No trust means no communication, which means no relationship. The person who develops the most productive relationships wins. In a happy marriage, both partners are happy doing things for one another. This develops a win-win situation in which both people are fulfilled.

Leaders are able to develop productive relationships with all kinds of people—whether they have similar social styles in the same matrix quadrant or not.

*"He who undervalues himself*
*is justly undervalued by others."*

—William Hazlitt

# Chapter Twenty-Six
# They Just Don't Understand

To further emphasize social styles and their importance in effective communication let's examine the cop-out excuse, "They just don't understand the way I feel. They just don't understand what I'm saying, how I think, what I want, what needs to be done." We blame others, but we need to take ownership of our miscommunication. If others don't understand us, it's our responsibility to do something about it.

The definition of effective communication is to convey clear meaning and obtain empathic understanding. I have modified the usual definition of communication to include it being our responsibility to convey that meaning and obtain that understanding. This eliminates our being able to say simply that others just don't understand. Now we responsibly say, "How can I say it so others will understand? It's not only the other people; it is I whose job it is to communicate effectively."

Instead of trying to get people to be satisfied with our own greatest wishes, wants, preferences and needs, we would benefit from appealing to other people's greatest needs—as defined by their particular social styles. This creates a truly productive relationship and stimulates people to do what we want them to do, while at the same time making them feel good about what they're doing.

Companies base their advertising campaigns to sell products or services upon these very social style needs. They tell their story to potential buyers according to the buyers' social style, the way they would most likely want to hear it.

How do we accomplish this? We can do this by learning the four basic needs that go with each social style. These are:

- Recognition (ego)
- Acceptance (relationships)
- Achievement (results)
- Being right (being secure in decisions)

If we look for these signs in the people with whom we have relationships, we can tell them things in the way that they want to be told. This is not a novel concept. We all have been told to place ourselves in other people's shoes before. Normally, this wisdom is utilized to invoke empathy and develop trust. In fact, when effectively communicating, we should always be putting ourselves in other people's shoes.

*"How many things would be different in everyone's surroundings if we hadn't lived? How a good word may have encouraged some fellow and done something to him that he did it differently and better than he would have otherwise. And through him somebody else was saved.*
*How much we contribute to each other.—How we each are—*
*And don't know it."*

—Rudolf Dreikurs

# Chapter Twenty-Seven
# How Powerful I Am

The "powerful you" is an extremely important aspect in your learning process on the journey to self-accountability. Although you can't change anybody but yourself, when you do change yourself that change has a profound impact on all the other people around you. The power of personal growth is contagious. Whatever you do to become better will influence others around you.

What we say and do has considerable impact on others if we decide to change and become more accountable. It will not only influence us and those with whom we come in contact, but it will also affect people we didn't even realize we could impact. Little things, like walking by someone in the office three or four times during the day and not acknowledging them, can be quite detrimental. This person might waste time and be less productive just worrying about how they might have displeased us. The vendor, our family, the stranger we pass on the street can all be affected by our attitude. If our attitude is positive, it becomes encouragingly contagious.

We stimulate others through their experience with us, and they in turn convey that experience to others and so on and so on. This can continue even as far as the neighbor's dog, who either receives a swift kick or a pat on the head, depending on how its owner has allowed him- or herself to be influenced that day.

I am firmly convinced that many of the health issues we face, such as stress and heart attacks, are a direct result of interpersonal frustration. We create complicated environments for ourselves by resisting the changes that could simplify our lives. The very issues that brought us to where we are now could be the very issues that land us squarely in the middle of nowhere.

We would all benefit from being more aware of power and allowing our attitudes and successes to have a positive effect on everyone we encounter.

*"Success requires no explanations:*
*failure permits no alibis."*

—Napoleon Hill

*"The measure of a man's success*
*is not the money he's made.*
*It's the kind of family he's raised."*

—Joseph P. Kennedy

# Part V
# I Had No Idea I Was This Good

On the journey to excellence in self-accountability, we will eventually find that we have become "unconsciously accountable" as the personal growth skills we have learned have become second nature.

* * * * *

McMaster Carr Supply Company, a mail-order catalog sales organization now doing a guestimated billion dollars in business a year, is owned by the Delaney family. I joined the company in 1966, after being recruited by Bob Delaney, its president. Bob was a typical example of someone with great humility who had held himself quite accountable. His father had brought him up to believe that the company's success had been arrived at more by luck than by purpose. Yet Bob had the insight to recognize that the company could achieve even greater success with more planning. There were opportunities and innovative approaches that hadn't been tested in mail-order, and Bob Delaney was willing to try some of them. This included new procedures for maintaining inventory control, receiving and processing mail and taking orders. With his ingenuity, he surrounded himself with people who had the foresight to go out and purchase a mainframe computer. The team complemented his humility, and achieved great success, while he continued to inspire the team and achieve results.

This is an example of how well people can do when they realize how talented they are and apply their gifts to their careers. They become unconsciously accountable in their business decisions, and great success follows.

* * * * *

People accuse me of being very lucky because all my children have turned out so well. I have a son who is a doctor, a daughter who is a physical therapist and another daughter who is raising my two very special grandchildren. Their accomplishments were not by accident. I believe the reason they were able to grow up and become responsible is because I dealt with myself. I was accountable to and for myself.

I created a situation in which I would come home and have dinner with the children. My then 13-year-old daughter would say, "Dad, have you had a bad day?" I would tell her it hadn't been all that bad and would ask her to sit down at the piano and sing for me. She would, beautifully, and still does when the opportunity arises. These things do not happen by themselves. They start with conveying to others that you have self-worth and consider yourself important and special in your own unique way and that you think they are too.

Once, when he thought I was out of earshot, "my son the doctor" was asked by a family friend in a humorous tone, "How did you three kids turn out to be so incredible with a father like yours?" His reply was, "It's very simple—fear." Well, I felt terrible, just terrible. But then my son quickly added, "No, I don't think it was fear at all. We just never wanted to disappoint him."

Now, you need to know that my children didn't grow up in the era of time-outs for misbehavior, but you also need to know that I didn't make a habit of spanking them either. There was a balance of discipline and nurturing. This all relates to thinking of each individual as being very special, the most special person in the whole world, according to his or her own particular style.

*"We know that if a person really
wants to be interested in others and
to work for the common cause,
he must first take care of himself.
He must have something to give
of himself, if the giving is
to mean anything."*

—Alfred Adler

# Chapter Twenty-Eight
# When Is It My Turn?

It's been your turn all the time, hasn't it? And the beauty of it is, it's still your turn and it's going to continue to be your turn. So by all means, take your turn. Don't wait for someone else to take your turn for you. Don't pass. Do it now.

One of my turns came when I was recruited by McMaster Carr Supply Company, which I previously mentioned. This company serves industrial, governmental and institutional organizations that use what are referred to as MRO (Maintenance, Repair and Operational) items—anything from hardware and tools to cranes and motors. After helping them revamp their inventory and distribution procedures, it was my turn to learn about computers. At that time I was still an unconsciously unaccountable fellow of thirty who had never heard of bytes, bits or cursors. I thought a cursor was someone who used swear words. But I went to IBM school and mastered the computer technology of the early 1970s. Through the use of this technology and continual development, McMaster was one of the first kids on the block to have a system so sophisticated that it could indicate when product was needed and where it was to be placed in the warehouse. Ninety percent of any order could be shipped on the day it was received—a milestone many companies would love to reach today!

This turn allowed me the opportunity to grow with a whole new group of people, catch up with them, pass them and ultimately (even without the last name Delaney) reach the level of corporate vice-president.

Be self-accountable. Your creator will undoubtedly admire your great faith and your trust in yourself as a result of cherishing and expressing your greatest gifts.

*"The journey of a thousand miles begins with one step."*

—Lao Tse

# Chapter Twenty-Nine
# Starting Is Half Done

If you say you will, then you're halfway there. In fact you're more than halfway there if you simply start on the journey toward change. Without beginning, you don't have a chance. If you've read this book and you've paid attention to what was shared, then you're halfway there because you've made a commitment to self-accountability. Think about how simple that is. I will and I do. It becomes a positive self-fulfilling prophecy. Tenacity and perseverance shine as you move forward. You are who you are mainly because of your efforts at self-obligation.

Every day we start a brand-new twenty-four-hour cycle. That's all we're allowed. Twenty-four hours. We have all kinds of resources at our disposal, but the most precious one of all is our time. The way we spend our time is too often very indiscriminate. We're not nearly as selective about how we spend our time as we are about the way we spend our money. We need to be sure we're budgeting our time wisely. And of course, not all twenty-four hours of a day are available to us. We have to eat, sleep and so forth.

So allot time to develop the skills necessary to achieve self-accountability. The time you say you never have is the time you'll gain by doing this. Take the time to have the time. It is just like planning.

Efficiency experts operate according to this concept. It's also important to make the best use of space available in work settings. It's critical to be able to do the job in the best way possible but in the least amount of time and space possible as well.

Expect that you can do this and you will. We move in line with our expectations—whether that line is crooked or askew, straight or curvy!

Recognize time as your most precious resource. Here is an exercise that requires the discipline you should follow in order to maximize your use of time:

For the next two weeks, keep track of and record how you are spending your time. Then prioritize your activities by first putting them in five or six categories and next ranking them within the categories in order of importance. Look for items that are your vital few in relation to your goals, both personal and career. Your trivial many become candidates for delegation and could become someone else's vital few. Look for items that you may not need to do anymore. After two weeks you will be surprised at how you are spending your time.

Next, develop time usage goals based on those

items that are vital toward meeting your goals. You will probably come up with four to six categories. Using 100 percent to represent total available time, assign a percentage of time to each one—a budget. Implement the plan to reach these time goals and continue to record how you are actually using your time.

Interruptions are a major cause of wasted time. Develop a strategy to manage these interruptions. For example, set aside specific times for others to come to you with less important issues. Use your telephone time wisely.

Spend your time as prudently as you budget your money. Evaluate decisions based on their time demands. Delegate all those things that you keep doing because you're concerned they won't be done or will be done poorly. Delegate the results you are expecting. Leave others to deal with the process. Maintain control; don't abdicate. This will negate the popular excuse, "By the time I tell someone what I want and how I want it done, I could have done it myself." Research has shown that the major deterrent to delegating is that we love doing things ourselves.

Continue to monitor how you are doing in comparison with your goals. Analyze significant difference. Every three to six months, go back to keeping the log of what you are actually doing.

This process works well for most people!

*"Nature has so arranged*
*the affairs of men that*
*strength grows out of struggle."*

—Napoleon Hill

# Chapter Thirty
# So How Do You Feel?

You should be a little bit uncomfortable by now, but feeling better! By now, you've learned how to be a little "positively insecure" because you have purposefully included it in your new paradigm plan. Knowingly go in and out of the wobblies and you've truly begun your journey of personal growth. As Josh Billings said, "Don't take the bull by the horns. Take him by the tail. Then you can let go when you want to."

For this book to have a positive impact on you, reevaluate who you are and why you're achieving less than you would like. Take the bull by the tail and be willing to accept the fact that you're going to have knots in your stomach and feel uncertain about whether this plan will work for you or whether you can do it. Can you cope with the fear of failing, the removal of the status quo, the invention of your future?

Be prepared for setbacks. Someone said, "They

told me to cheer up—things could be worse. I cheered up and, sure enough, things got worse." As the song goes, "Pick yourself up, dust yourself off and start all over again." If this whole process were easy, you would have already done it. On the way to getting to where you're going, which is different from where you are now, you'll run into some stumbling blocks. These will provide marvelous excuses to stop:

- "I've been doing this for a month, and I haven't received a raise."
- "I'm not cut out for this."
- "I've tried it, but it hasn't made that much difference."
- "No one's even noticed my effort."
- "I'm getting no recognition or respect."

There are always all these things to deal with, and the issue always comes back to personal growth. You have to continue to experience personal growth, by which I mean an ongoing structured program of identifying what you're really good at and what you have to do to get better at what you're not good at. Be prepared for the adversity that goes along with overcoming the barriers you face. You can't get to the other side without fighting adverse currents.

*"Lord, grant me patience—but hurry!"*
—Unknown

In the words of Evan Esar, "There is no shortcut to success. If you want to get to the Promised Land, you must go through the wilderness." Believe that you can do it and use that as the strength to continue on. You will overcome the setbacks. And as Leo Buscaglia says, "When you're at the end of your rope, grab hold and swing."

## Who Said This Was Going to Be Hard?

In penning this book, I was fortunate to receive input from some valued colleagues. As with all suggestions, I listened, made my assessment and then acted by either agreeing and making it so or disagreeing and continuing on the path.

One particular recommendation was to develop a step-by-step plan to teach someone how to reach a level of self-accountability. I listened and evaluated the suggestion, but something about it didn't seem right. My colleague may have lost sight of the fact that becoming self-accountable and putting one's dreams in action is very personal and unique to any individual. By following a step-by-step approach that is developed by me, you are already becoming self-*un*accountable and accountable to my plan for you.

What I have provided for you in this book are tools, concepts and awareness that you can consider utilizing on your road to self-accountability.

Let me now review a few of those key points...

1. Continue to ask yourself, What is it I do? Don't forget to listen carefully to your answer.
2. Get to know yourself. Evaluate your strengths

and weaknesses. Maintain a success book. You are your best cheerleader.

3. Welcome change. Remember: no wobblies, no growth; no growth, no fulfillment.

4. Remain focused on the vital few; ignore the trivial many.

5. Prioritize your worry list.

6. Your cure for victimitis is inventing your future.

7. Formulate a plan for growth. Set goals with deadlines to s-t-r-e-t-c-h beyond your comfort zones.

8. Perception is reality—the only person you can change is yourself.

9. Accept the responsibility of communications. Remember: "Say and do unto others as they would want you to say and do unto them."

10. Become self-accountable.

* * * * *

Most of what you've learned is pretty simple. But remember, it all comes down to one basic principle that can change your life forever, regardless of what other people do: hold yourself accountable. It's the right thing to do to get where you want to go, and the rewards are worth it!

*"To accomplish great things, we must not only act but dream, not only plan but also believe."*
—Anatole France

# You Are Not Alone

There's a lot we all can learn about leadership and personal growth from each other. If you have an interesting story of how you've made anything possible in your life, I would love to hear it. And if you're interested in consulting services, on either an individual or group basis, or are looking for a speaker for a convention or organization, or would simply like to find out about other products, services and workshops that are available to help you on your journey to self-accountability and self-discovery, please contact me at the following address.


Al Marino
Leadership Resources Institute
2251 North Rampart Boulevard
Las Vegas, NV 89128
(702) 458-5355